Sweet

Hearts

Sweet Hearts

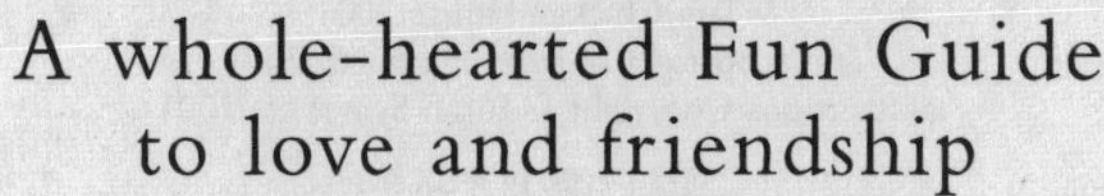

A whole-hearted Fun Guide
to love and friendship

Janet Hoggarth
Illustrated by Sarah Symonds

The Chicken House
An Egmont joint venture

To Pete Benn, the love of my life (!)
and all my friends –
it'd be boring without you.

First published in Great Britain in 2001
This edition published in 2002
by The Chicken House,
2 Palmer Street, Frome, Somerset BA11 1DF, UK

ISBN 1 90343407 6

British Library Cataloguing in Publication data available.
Library of Congress Cataloguing in Publication data available.

Printed and bound in Denmark by Nørhaven Paperback A/S

Contents

There are recipes in this book that need a bit of help from a friendly grown-up!

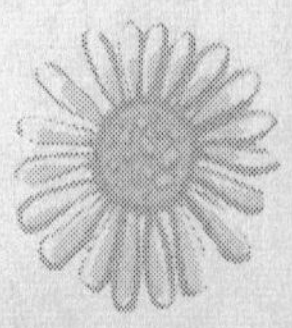

Introduction

Life is nothing without friendship.
Cicero

Love and friendship — a quick low-down

Love and friendship — it's cool! Love makes the world go round, doesn't it? And without our friends, school, home, and life would be sooooooo boring. The best thing about having friends is that you always have someone to turn to who knows you better than anyone.

You can moan about anything *(zzzz)* and they will listen, give you great advice *(Stop whining!)*, and then cheer you up by making you laugh *(You've got a huge zit on your nose...)*. Friends are the best — you help and understand each other and have fun at the

same time. What more could you ask for?

Though we love our friends, we are not *in* love with them. Being *in* love is a different pair of shoes altogether. Love can be all hearts and flowers and presents and surprises (umm ... yeah, right!). It is all of those things — honest! But not all of the time — in the famous words of Shakespeare "The course of true love never did run smooth." Falling in love is really like elephants trampolining in your tummy, coupled with a brain on melt-down. Everyday life goes out the window — your only thought is your crush! You are

watching *The Simpsons* and Bart suddenly turns into ... *him*. You are in English — forget essays, all you can write is his name over and over again.

If he loves you back — that's cool and you can both feel sick together, but have all the nice stuff too. However, if he doesn't know

you feel like this and you want to tell him, why not try some of the ideas in this book — let him know how you feel. You might find out he is feeling too sick to eat chocolate, too!

1

Hanging Out

Real friendship is shown in times of trouble; prosperity is full of friends.
Euripedes

Friends — what do they mean to you? Everything, probably. Laughing and chilling out were invented to do with friends. So was chowing down bars and bars of chocolate and take-out pizzas by the truckload. Moaning about boys is also a headliner, but there's a lot more to friendship than that.

What makes a good friend?

What do you think are the vital ingredients for a friend you want to hang out with?

"You can tell them everything without getting embarrassed."

Kerry, 16

"They would probably forgive me if I did something wrong." Stephanie, 11

"They are only a phone call away and are there for the good times and the bad." Heather, 16

"You are able to tell them secrets and know they will keep them." Victoria, 11

"They stick up for me and help me with school work." Danny, 8

"They know when you need to be left alone." Abi, 11

Hold a true friend with both hands. Nigerian proverb

Add your own thoughts in these bubbles.

FORGIVE
Sharing

Is she worth her weight in chocolate?

Whiz through this quiz to see if your friend is the right chocolate bar for you.

1. You are both up for the lead in the school play and you get the part. Would she:

(a) Give you a big hug and offer to help you with your lines?

(b) Stomp off in a huff and not speak to you for a week?

(c) Be disappointed and be all quiet for a few hours, then snap out of it and say congrats?

2. It is the big school dance and you are wearing a particular glittery top that you bought specially. She turns up in the same one. Would she:

(a) Laugh hysterically and suggest you stay together all night as a glitter overload?

(b) Stomp off and go home to change? At least she didn't make you do it.

(c) Insist that you wear your sweatshirt over it, as she doesn't have hers with her?

3. She finds out that a boy likes you, but the only problem is that she liked him first. Would she:

(a) Never tell you, hoping that he will move on to her or someone else?

(b) Hurtle up to you at a million miles an hour and spill the beans at top speed?

(c) Eventually tell you after finding out how he felt about her?

4. You have forgotten to do your History homework and the teacher is super strict. Detention looms. Would she:

(a) Help you think up an excuse for the sympathy vote?

(b) Shrug and say she had detention last week for not doing it, too? Chill out.

(c) Give you her homework to copy but ask you to change a few words here and there?

5. You've not been invited to the class Princess's birthday mega-do but she has. Would she:

(a) Not go – what would be the point if she couldn't do stupid dance routines with her partner in crime?

(b) Say that she really wanted to go and hoped you didn't mind, but if you did, she wouldn't go.

(c) Go anyway and bring you back a squashed piece of cake?

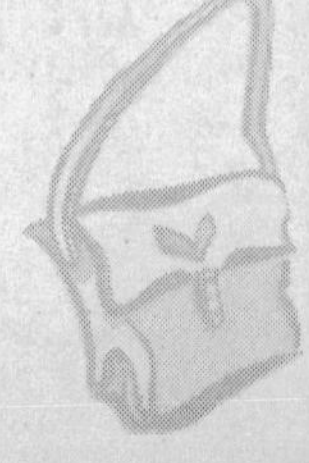

Scores on the doors

1. a) 3 b) 1 c) 2
2. a) 3 b) 2 c) 1
3. a) 1 b) 3 c) 2
4. a) 2 b) 1 c) 3
5. a) 3 b) 2 c) 1

So - what chocolate bar is she?

Giant Toblerone 12 - 15 points

You friend is the ultimate in chocolate bars – just right for you. Pure like Swiss chocolate, she will always be true to you and help you out.

Underneath the chocolate hides yummy honey and exciting crispy almond, meaning that she sweetly puts others first, but loves a good time, as long as it's with you.

Snickers 7 - 11 points

Covered in milk chocolate but packs a punch – sound familiar? Biting into the bar, you come across all sorts, just like her. Crunchy peanuts get

stuck in your teeth – a bit like her moods. But the creamy nougat and caramel cancel it out – she will make up for any unfriendly behavior by sweet-talking you.

Any low calorie bar 5–7 points

At first glance the milk chocolate covering makes you want to buy it, but when you bite in, you find there is nothing but air. All surface and no

substance – that's your friend. She thinks about herself too much, and if she's not careful, you'll toss her aside for a tastier bar ... uhh ... friend.

The friendship fitness test

Now you know what sort of sassy chicks your friends are, but what about you? I think we'd better make sure you pass the friends fitness test or you might have to put in a serious bout of training...

1. It's your best friend's birthday so you celebrate this special day by:

(a) Making her a fab present from the present ideas in this book and a handmade card.

(b) Forgetting – you remembered last year, didn't you?

(c) Telling the boys in your class it's her birthday so they tease her on the playground.

2. She tells you a really important secret that must never be repeated. Do you:

(a) Promise to never tell, even if bribed by Leonardo Di Caprio with a big kiss?

(b) Tell the school blabbermouth? Oops.

(c) Tell another close friend by mistake – you forgot you weren't supposed to.

❸ Your friend is getting ready to go out on her first date with the boy you secretly like. Do you:

(a) Tell her she looks better than Britney and hope she has a wicked time?

(b) Wish her a fab evening, but secretly hope he hates those pants you said made her look thin?

(c) Tell her that the film they are going to see is terrible and you think he's a loser to have chosen it?

4. You are just on your way out to meet the school heartthrob in the park with another friend when your best bud calls in tears; she needs you to come over *now*. Do you:

(a) Say you'll come right over? You can't bear to hear her so upset.

(b) Say you are so sorry, but you've got to go and visit your granny and are just walking out the door.

(c) Ask her what the problem is and sort it out on the phone, telling her you are going out.

5. She got a disastrous hair cut that makes her look like a boy (eek!). Do you:

(a) Give her all your hair products, clips, studs, butterflies and transform her into a popstar?

(b) Think – yes! Now I will look better than her for a change?

(c) Laugh wildly and then apologize like mad, saying it's not that bad?

Results please, nurse
Mostly As

Seriously dedicated as a friend – that's you. Nothing gets in the way of you helping out in a crisis, but be careful not to overdo it and end up exhausted. Slow down and put yourself first occasionally. You pass with flying colors.

Mostly Bs

You are so out of condition that you'd better get back into training now! You need to do a set of sympathy push-ups and a fast circuit of good will around the track. You have potential if only you'd just think about your actions before you say or do anything.

Mostly Cs

You are a good friend, most of the time, but can mess up a lot, like most of us. Perhaps a few more circuits around the tactful comments arena might sort you out. You don't mean any harm; it's just that your tongue runs away with you sometimes.

It's all in the stars

Are you and your friends (and boyfriend) a match made in heaven or a disaster waiting to happen? Why is it that some people get along and others don't? Could it have anything to do with your inner selves connecting? (Heavy, or what!?)

See what kind of dudettes you are and if you are a perfect match for each other. Check out your boyfriend's stars too!

Aries – *popular (March 21–April 20)*

You love adventure, partying, and anything new. A loyal and generous friend, you like

your friends to be as courageous as you are. You tend to show off a bit too!
Special understandings with: Sagittarians and other Aries.

Taurus – *loyal (April 21–May 20)*
You are laid-back, kind, and extremely charming. You only lose your temper if seriously pushed. Once you've adopted someone, you're friends for life.
Special understandings with: Virgos, Capricorns, and Taureans.

Gemini – *magnetic (May 21–June 20)*
You are amusing, entertaining, and attract friends easily. People instantly feel comfortable with you. However, you tire of things and people very easily.
Special understandings with: Aquarians, Librans, and Geminis.

Cancer – *a rock (June 21–July 20)*
You are a very homey person who likes nothing better than hiding away from the big wide world. A caring sensitive friend, you are ready to lend a hand at any time.
Special understandings with: Scorpios, Pisces, and Cancerians.

Leo – *warm (July 21–August 20)*
A born leader, you like to dominate the scene and get attention! But you make a loving friend who will do anything for your pals — as long as they respect you. **Special understandings with:** Aries, Sagittarians, and Leos.

Virgo – *vibrant (Aug 21–Sept 22)*
Witty and reliable — that's you. You don't like lying or being messed with, but love helping other people out of a jam. **Special understandings with:** Taureans, Capricorns, and Virgos.

Libra – *sharer (Sept 23–Oct 22)*
You have a habit of ignoring problems, but when it comes to friends you'll do anything to stop an argument. You love sharing and hate letting people down.
Special understandings with: Geminis, Aquarians, and Librans.

Scorpio – *sparky (Oct 23–Nov 22)*
A fascinating and mysterious person, you choose your friends very carefully. You're brilliant at keeping secrets. But you will not let on if you have a problem.
Special understandings with: Cancerians, Pisceans, and Scorpios.

Sagittarius – *adventurous (Nov 23–Dec 20)*
Wow! Everyone wants to be your friend — you are fun and completely trustworthy. However you can be too outspoken, often saying the wrong thing.
Special understandings with: Aries, Leos, and Sagittarians.

Capricorn – *intense (Dec 21–Jan 19)*
You tend to be serious and don't let your hair down much. Quite shy, you can take a while to make friends. When you do, you are kind and generous forever.
Special understandings with: Taureans, Virgos, and Capricorns.

Aquarius – *in demand (Jan 20–Feb 18)*
An original is what you are — always surprising everyone. Very supportive, you accept people for what they are. With so many friends you have trouble seeing them all.
Special understandings with: Geminis, Librans, and Aquarians.

Pisces – *adored (Feb 19–March 20)*
Your natural creativity and sense of freedom make you a popular friend to have. You always know how people are feeling and allow others to be themselves.
Special understandings with: Cancerians and other Pisceans.

How to handle fall outs

◆ Always talk to another friend about it first and get another point of view. You might find out something useful.

◆ If you know deep down it is your fault, be honest and apologize as soon as you can, then she can't brood about it too much.

◆ If it was her fault that you fell out, don't scream and demand an apology. Ask her why she did it. There might be some misunderstanding you knew nothing about.

◆ If you find yourself being ignored by someone in your group of friends, stay cool about it (if you can) and get one of them on their own and find out why.

◆ If you notice someone in your group is being ignored, don't join in. How would you like it?

◆ Do not take it all so seriously, be calm, and do something else for a while. It will probably have blown over by the time you get to hang out again.

◆ To call a truce, make a present and give it to her — she can hardly be upset after that, can she?

◆ Accept that friends aren't perfect and will make mistakes — we all do. You will find next time you get mad about it, it might make it easier.

◆ Finally, always forgive and forget because holding a grudge can ruin any great friendship.

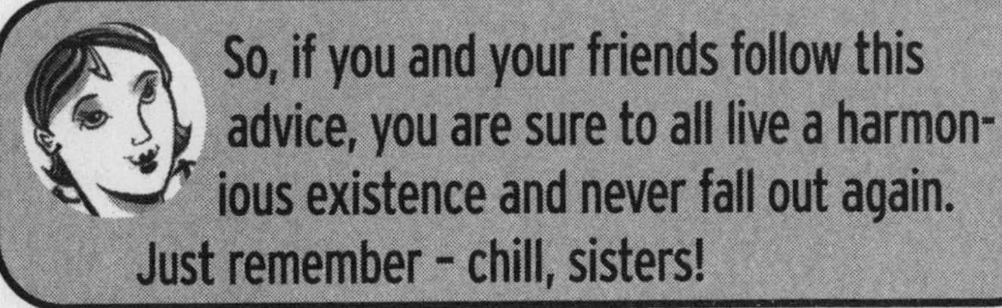

2
Pajama Parties

Sleepovers, slumber parties, pajama parties, whatever you want to call them, they are cool and a good way to have fun with all your friends in one place at the same time.

You obviously do have to ask permission first because it will be your 'rents who have to stay up all night and listen to your hysterical giggles at the latest movie and your screaming as you tell each other ghost stories.

Top ten list of basics needed for the Big Night:

1. Lots of sleep the night before – you have to stay awake for a long time!
2. Your gang of best buddies handpicked by you.

3. Your fave nightshirt or pajamas and a big sleeping bag.
4. Instant camera to capture those goofy faces and chocolate-covered mouths.
5. Piles of popcorn, sweets, and special sleep-over recipes AND breakfast!

6. Drinks. Soda and orange juice aside – make fruit cocktails from the recipe section too.
7. Face mask ingredients and tons of make-up, nail polish, and tattoos – go tattoo crazy!
8. Lots of pens and paper.

9. Special videos, lots of magazines, games, dice, CDs.
10. Flashlight for when it's Lights Out and you want to keep talking.

Munchie must haves

You can choose from some of the recipes in the recipe section, or you can make your own stuff. Or you could have personalized mini heart pizzas, which are super easy to make. Make sure there is a grown-up on hand to help.

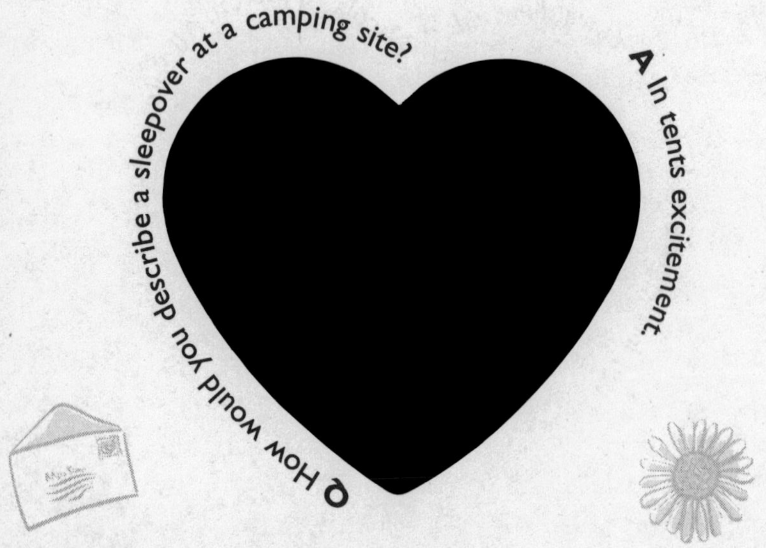

Personal mini heart pizzas

Two packs of dough mix — three if you are having more than five people. It should specify on the pack how many people it will serve.

One 14oz (400g) can chopped tomatoes
Two cloves garlic chopped
One medium onion chopped
One tablespoon tomato puree
Two tablespoons oil
One teaspoon each dried oregano, sugar
Handful corn meal

Heart-shaped cookie cutter
Various toppings: sliced tomatoes, onions, mushrooms, peppers, pineapple, ham, salami, tuna, sweetcorn, grated cheese, and whatever else you love.

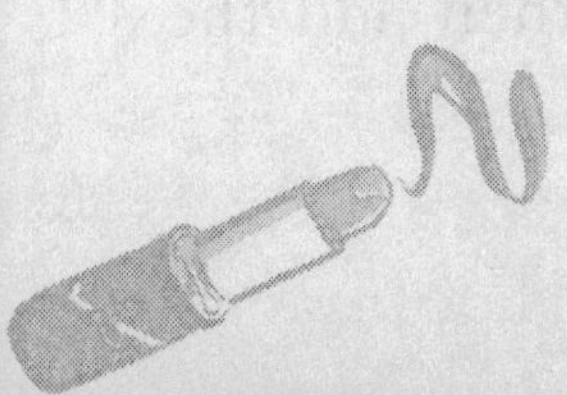

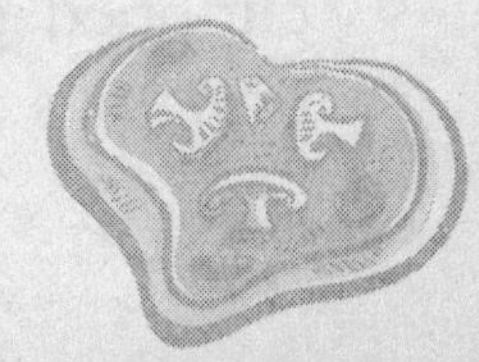

❖ Preheat the oven to 425°F (220°C). Make the dough according to the packet instructions.

❖ Add the oil to a pan and heat up gently. Then add the onion with a pinch of salt. Fry for about five minutes with the chopped garlic and oregano, then add the tomatoes and puree.

❖ Let that all cook for a couple more minutes then add the brown sugar. Keep stirring and then leave to simmer while you roll out the dough for the crusts.

❖ You need to separate the dough into as many pieces as there are going to be people at your sleepover.

❖ Roll each one into a ball then roll flat with a rolling pin. You want it to be about a quarter of an inch thick before you stop rolling.

❖ Use a cookie cutter to make heart-shaped dough crusts, sprinkle cornmeal over one side of each crust and then lay the cornmeal sides on the baking sheet. Spread a layer of sauce on the crusts and then sprinkle with cheese.

❖ Now this is where you have to personalize each pizza. Grab the topping ingredients and get creative. The initials of each of your friends can be spelled out on each pizza in slices of peppers, mushrooms, whatever.

You can carve them out of ham, dot them out in sweetcorn, or squash them out in tuna! Yum.

❖ Put the trays in the oven for about ten to fifteen minutes and presto! pizzas ready to munch while watching videos or gossiping about the latest boy band. Enjoy. Serve with spicy fries (see page 126).

Edible jewelry

As well as chocolate, cakes, and ice-cream for dessert, you could make an edible necklace. All you need is popcorn, jelly beans, fruit snacks, or any soft candy. Get a needle and

thread and gather your selection of goodies around you. Poke the needle through the middle of them and keep threading as many as you can on the thread, in different combinations. Tie the ends together to make a cool edible treat that could double up as a . . . um ... stylish (yeah, right!) piece of jewelry.

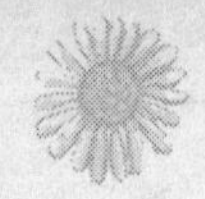

How to make yourself and your friends look like babes

After pigging out you might need to relax a bit and let your food settle, so why not chill and do some homemade face masks to make you all look like princesses.

Oily skin

Put one egg white and three drops of lemon juice in a bowl and whisk with a fork, but not so much that it turns into meringue. Apply to your face with a pastry brush. Cut off slices of cucumber and place carefully over each eye. Now lie back and relax! Rinse off after

ten minutes with warm water and smile because your skin looks like a supermodel's.

Dry skin

If you think you have dry skin, try this one. Take the leftover egg yolk and a spoonful of honey and mix well in a bowl. Put it on your

face with a pastry brush and lie back with cucumber slices in place over your eyes. Drape a plastic bag around your chin as your mask could slide off and make a nice icky mess on your shirt. After ten minutes, rinse it off with warm water. Can you see a difference?

Just for fun

Mash up an avocado with a tablespoon each of lemon juice, honey, and natural yogurt and leave it to set for thirty minutes. Slap that on your face for ten minutes and rinse off with cool water. It makes your skin soft while you just look like an alien. Nice one!

Do I look gorgeous now?

Your skin is glowing — it's time to enhance it even more with some uhh . . . catwalk make-up.

✖ Take turns doing a different feature on one of you — i.e. eyes, cheeks, lips, nails . . .

✖ Go crazy — use all different colors, false eyelashes, glitter, bindis, bronzers, liquid eye–shadows, powder, eye-liner, colored mascara, and hair mascara. More glitter anyone?

✖ No one is allowed to use the same color twice and no one is to look until the final touch has been added.

✖ Don't forget to add tattoos — they look cool on ankles and shoulder blades.

No cheating please

As well as Twister and Pictionary, there are other games you can try at your sleepover.

tattoos

"All my friends are confident and fun." Roberta, 11

The Chocolate Race

If you can possibly fit any more food in, play this game.

★ You will need the hugest bar of your favorite chocolate, a wool hat, a pair of gloves, a scarf, a knife and fork, and a pair of dice.

★ Sit in a circle on the floor with all the things in the middle and one person starts off by rolling the dice. If they don't get a double, pass to the next person until someone does get a double.

★ Oh no! You got the double! Rush to the center and put on the hat, gloves, and scarf, and try to eat the chocolate with a knife and fork. (It sounds easy. It's not.)

★ All the time the dice is going around, and the second another player gets a double, your

chance to stuff any more chocolate is over. Boo hoo. Take off all the clothes and go back to the circle and watch jealously as this player manages to eat more than you . . .

★ You can play this until you run out of chocolate or feel very, very sick — it's up to you!

Make your own boy

This is not very kind, but we love it!

★ You'll need all your magazines for this. What you are looking for is a couple of full-size poster pics of some guys — soap stars, boy bands, whatever you like.

★ You might want to do this before everyone arrives to save time. Mount each picture on some thin card. Wait for it to dry and then carefully cut them out.

★ Make surgical snips and cut off their heads, legs and arms. Ow! Mount the headless

torsos on two separate pieces of card with enough room surrounding them to add the arms, legs, and heads and attach to the wall with Fun Tack or pins.

★ Now stick Fun Tack to the back of each limb and head, mix up the body parts in a

hat, and you are ready to play the game.

★ Blindfold two friends and make them select dismembered bits from the hat. They might need a bit of help finding the torso on the wall, but apart from that — no helping!

★ It's no surprise to hear that the winner is the one who creates the nearest resemblance to a human being! Oh boys, watch out . . .

As well as games, you could all make gifts from other chapters in this book.

The morning after the night before

You've stayed up all night. So what's a girl to eat after such a hectic night in? You could try these mega-quick recipes that have been making the rounds at sleepovers for decades . . .

Cinnamon toastie

★ Find a loaf of bread and toast a whole load under the grill, but only on one side!

★ Turn over when done and spread with butter. Sprinkle with cinnamon and brown

sugar and then pop back under the grill until all the sugar has crystallized. Eat right away.

French toast

★ You will need two eggs per person. Beat in a bowl with a splash of milk.

★ Heat a frying pan with some butter and make sure it covers the bottom nicely.

★Get dipping! The bread that is — into the egg mixture. Place carefully in the pan and brown both sides.

★ Serve either with maple syrup, lemon and honey, ketchup, bacon — the list is endless.

Oh, what a night!

You've survived your sleepover. No one fought, no one was sick (unless they ate all the pizzas), and now you must give away little reminders of your oh-so-cool Big Night In.

You could buy everyone a small gift like glossy new lipstick, nail polish, tattoos – or you could make them something from elsewhere in this book (see chapter four)

BUDDIES

3
The one about Boys

'Tis better to have loved and lost
Than never to have loved at all.
Alfred, Lord Tennyson

Hubba hubba! You've got a crush on Matt in your class, but does he like you? You feel sick if he looks at you and chocolate has lost its appeal. You dream about him holding your hand and taking you in his arms and uhh . . . enough of that! Listen — did you read the quote at the top of the page? Girl, we do not

have to wait for boys to ask us out, we go for it and ask them ourselves! If you never try, you'll never know and will wonder forever more, "What if . . ."

"If I see a boy I like, I try to get a bit of eye contact and look as if I'm having a really good time." Billie Piper

Open his eyes

But before you go in full force you'd better make sure he knows you exist!

✸ If you know there is an after school club your boy belongs to, join it — even if it is not your thing.
✸ Make eye contact in class and when you have held his gaze for a few seconds, look away. Works every time!
✸ Smile at him! It is easy and it costs nothing.

A smile can change someone's day. Let's hope it's yours.
✸ At lunch, you could sit near him in the cafeteria and get out those cakes you made for all your friends. Share with him, too, of course!
✸ If you know his e-mail address (be devious

and find out) you could send him an e-crush message. Log on here: **www.ecrush.com/** and the site will send him a message saying someone has a crush on him. He won't know it's you — you work that out after he responds.

After all that smiling and eye contact, have you planted the seed of love in his brain? Complete this mini quiz to see if he's hitting on you or is still in love with his football.

1. You are in the bus to school and he sits next to you. Would he:

(a) Ask you to help him with his math homework – it is your best subject after all.

(b) Go completely red after grunting something that could have been "hi"?

(c) Ignore you completely and read his soccer mag?

2. You walk by in the playground with your friends and he's with his. Would he:

(a) Ask if you girls want to hear any rude jokes?

(b) Smile and say hi while his friends snicker into their sandwiches?

(c) Not even look up from the game of soccer he's playing with his friends?

3. You have to work with him in a French oral test. Would he:

(a) Spill his guts and tell you he is into someone else?

(b) Tease you mercilessly about your pronunciation while not looking you in the eye?

(c) Just take the test without much small talk?

4. You see him in McDonalds while you're with your cousin Andy. Would he:

(a) Give you a friendly wave on the way out?

(b) Nod hello and on Monday ask who was that boy you were with?

(c) Blank you as usual. You may as well be a potted plant.

Results:

Mostly As

He likes you, but not in the way you want him to. He sees you as a friend, someone he can talk to about other girls and mess around with. Be his buddy – you never know it could blossom into something else, but don't hold out for it.

Mostly Bs

He has a crush on you as big as a football field. The fact that he can't talk to you without blushing or being a stammering wreck are all signs that he likes you like mad. Go, girl! End his misery – ask him out now!

Mostly Cs

Don't even waste time on this guy. He doesn't know you exist, he probably doesn't realize any girl exists. Leave him to his soccer and give up. Look out for that cute boy in the class next door instead.

Top tips on getting a date and how to cope if he says no (get real!)

✲ Be very relaxed (not easy, but you can pretend!) and do not be afraid to look him in the eye when you do it.

"The best thing a friend ever did for me was to ask a boy to go out with me." Jodie, 10

✲ Make sure none of your friends are around as there is nothing worse than a gaggle of giggling girls in the background.

✲ Suggest something really casual like going to the movies with a group or on your own (eek!); or meeting in town at McDonalds; or ask him to come over to your house to play the latest computer game/surf the Net.

✲ If he says no, it is NO BIG DEAL! Just shrug and go "OK, just thought it would be fun" or something like that. I bet he won't though if he likes you.

✲ Do not get down if he says no. It is soooooo not worth it. I know you may feel stupid and feel like everyone knows. They don't! Anyway, he just hasn't realized yet what a cool, beautiful, and caring person you are.

✲ Act like nothing has happened — like you never asked him out. You don't want him and

anyone else to think he's rocked your universe, do you? Matt who?

The Big Date

So, he said yes (!) and you are going on a date with him to . . . let's say . . . the movies. But what are you going to wear? What will you

talk about? What if he tries to kiss you? Take a chill pill and remember these pointers:

✲ Wear something you know you look good in and have worn before. There is no point wearing your dancing outfit and a tube top. You want to be comfortable and not scare the poor boy off!

✲ He will be nervous, too. You can bet that he is checking his armpits for sweat marks as he leaves his house!

✲ Who pays? You both do — this is what is known as going Dutch.

✲ Do not worry that you'll have nothing to talk about — that is why the movies were invented. They're a great first date because all you have to cope with is ordering the popcorn and before you know it, it's time to go in.

✲ If he tries to kiss you in the dark and you don't want to, do not freak, just tell him "Not yet." That isn't a total rejection but it says enough — that you aren't ready.

Dr. Jeykll and Mr. Hyde

You've hung out together a few times after your date and then suddenly he starts acting weird. One minute you are the best, the next minute he's walking right past you in the lunch line without even a nod. Helloooo? *What is his problem?*

★ He could be being teased by friends for going out with a girl, so in front of them he has to blank you to keep his image. Not cool, but boys are like that.

★ He might not know how he feels about you and instead of talking to you about it, he is ignoring you till he feels sure.

★ He could like you and is scared you don't like him as much, so by ignoring you he shows he doesn't care, and if you dump him, his heart won't be crushed into a million pieces! Boys!

★ He could be doing the coward thing and dumping you without telling you. What a sleaze. Boys sometimes don't want to face up to saying those words: "I don't want to go out with you any more."

Boys are famous for not talking about feelings and girls are famous for wanting to talk about nothing else, so be a girl and find out why he is Rude Boy. Then do something about it. You might want to finish it, if so read on . . .

You're history!

Being dumped or dumping someone is not nice. If you feel like you don't like your guy any more, that's fine. Don't keep going out with him for the sake of it — that's not fair.

Q Why did the chocolate chip cookie cry?

A Because he had been forced to break up.

★ Always try and do it face to face. By phone or letter is the coward's way out.

★Do not do it in public. Arrange to meet somewhere quiet and just say what's on your mind.

★Never let him find out from gossip — it is

humiliating and how would you like it?

★ If he treats you badly afterward, it is just his wounded ego barking. Accept it and don't rise to any comments he throws your way. He just isn't as mature as you, obviously!

If you are the dumpee and you feel humiliated and hurt, it is tempting to get revenge by doing something evil or flirting with his best friend, but in the end, he is not worth it.

★ Act cooler than an ice cube at a freezer convention and swan around like a princess.

★ Be a girl and talk about how you feel with all your friends. That is a huge help and stops you from brooding about it.

★ Write a letter to him and vent all your bad feelings and anger BUT do not send it. Chuck it in the trash along with all the hurt you feel. He will soon be in your memory pail.

Boys as friends?

Is this possible? I bet you have at least one boy you would call a friend. Just because a boy is your bud, it doesn't mean you like each other. Boy buds are great because:

a) They are not going to wear the same clothes as you to a party or copy your

intricately braided new hairstyle.

b) They don't sit and moan about boys to you. They might moan about girls, but I doubt it. Girls are perfect!

c) If you like someone, a boy friend can find out through the boy grapevine if you have a chance with him quicker than a girl friend could.

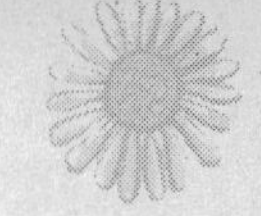

d) You can sound them out with your boy troubles and get the guy point of view.
e) You might pick up a different interest or discover something new about you that wouldn't have come to the surface with your girlie posse.

Maybe you don't want a boyfriend and are just not ready yet, so make a new friend instead. Go forth and get yourself one today!

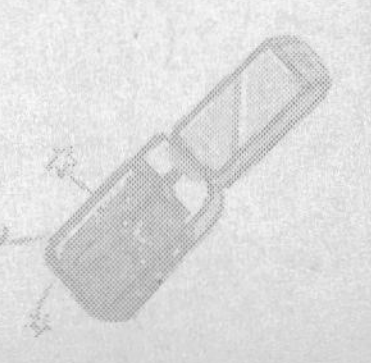

4

Valentine Wishes

All you need to know about the big day

What is Valentine's day? We all know that it is the day that lovers and friends exchange gifts and cards to celebrate love and friendship, but

how did it come about? And who was this dude Saint Valentine anyway?

Saint Valentine — this is your life!

Valentine was a priest in Rome during the third century. The city was ruled by Emperor Claudius, who banned people from getting

married. He thought that if men remained single with no wives or children, they would join the army and help him conquer other countries. How wrong he was!

Romeo, Romeo, wherefore art thou Romeo? Juliet from *Romeo and Juliet*

This is where our hero Valentine comes into the picture. He secretly wed people who were in love. However, one night he got caught and was thrown in prison — his punishment was death. "No way!" everyone

cried, but nothing could save him. One story about Valentine said he fell in love with the jailer's daughter, and on the day of his death (February 14th — the day before the Roman love festival Lupercalia) he left her a note saying "Love from your Valentine." But no one really knows — there could have been more than one

Valentine and over the years all the stories melted into one. Eventually, in 496 AD, Pope Gelasius made February 14 a day for remembering Saint Valentine and celebrating love and friendship.

Valentine facts

☆Long ago, the liver — not the heart — was the part of the body that symbolized love.

☆ In the Middle Ages, young men and women drew names from a bowl to see who their Valentine would be. They would wear these names on their sleeves for one week.

☆ It was believed that if a woman saw a robin flying overhead on Valentine's day, it meant she would marry a sailor. If she saw a sparrow, she would marry a poor man, and a goldfinch meant a millionaire. What if she saw a 747?

☆ In Wales, wooden love spoons were carved and given on February 14. Hearts, keys, and

keyholes were favorite decorations meaning, "You unlock my heart."

So we know about Valentine, but there is also another fellow involved in love...

And as for that guy Cupid . . .

The chubby cherub hails from Roman mythology. In Latin, the language of ancient Rome, the word cupido means desire.

As the son of Venus the goddess of love, Cupid shoots arrows tipped with gold. Those

struck by the arrows would fall in love. Ouch! Just be on the lookout for that cherub. He might be striking at a school near you soon!

This is a good time of year to tell the boy you're crushing on how you feel with a card or gift.

Giant Heart Cookies

This is a funky idea to send instead of a card. You can also make mini hearts with a heart-shaped pastry cutter.

1½oz (40g) butter
3oz (75g) brown sugar

8oz (225ml) syrup
2fl oz (50ml) cold water
14oz (400g) plain flour
Half a teaspoon salt
Half a teaspoon each of ground ginger and cinnamon
One teaspoon baking soda
One tablespoon cold water

❖Heat oven to 350°F (180°C).
❖Mix the butter, sugar, and syrup with the 2 fl oz of water in a bowl.
❖Sift the flour, salt, and spices together and stir into the syrup mixture.
❖Dissolve the soda in the tablespoon of

water and stir in, too. Leave the dough to chill for a bit.

❖Roll it out about half of an inch (one centimeter) thick.

❖Now make a heart template out of cardboard and cut very carefully around it. You can make it as big as you like. If you want to bake

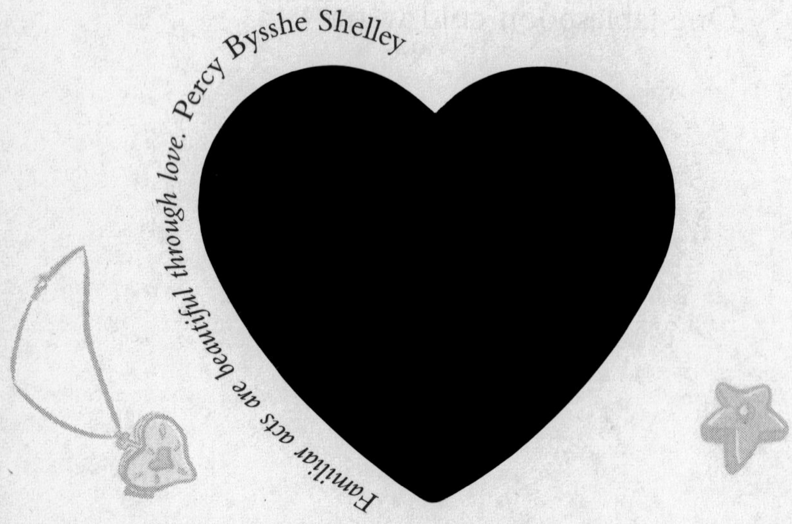

a message into the cookie, press in raisins to spell out your words.

❖Any leftover scraps can be re-rolled and made into small heart-shaped cookies.

❖Bake in the oven for about fifteen minutes. When completely cool decorate with love

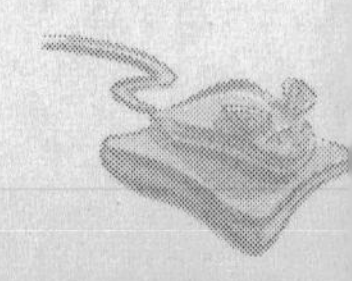

messages in squeezy icing. You can buy all different colors.

Top tip!

If you bake this for a friend as a special thank you, before you put the cookie in the oven, roll up a piece of foil into a ball, then surround it

with greaseproof paper. Cut a hole about a half of an inch (one centimeter) in diameter and one inch (two centimeters) from the top of the heart and place the ball in there. When the cookie has cooled, take out the ball and you have a hole through which you can thread red ribbon and hang the heart from it.

Cheezy tunes card

Another way to send a card that isn't a card is to make your chosen Valentine a compilation tape of their favorite tracks — but disguise it!

Stuff to buy:

Blank tape
Plain card — not too thick

Sticky pads that you use in photo albums or double-sided sticky tape
Red foil paper (just an idea)

✪ If you're in synch with your Valentine, you will know their fave tunes. Once you've laid down the tracks in the recording studio (your bedroom) on to the tape *(you are the DJ!)*,

it's time to rock!

✪ Cut your card to any size bigger than the tape. Make a one-inch (two-centimeter) wide section down the center of the card and then score each side of this with a knife. This gives your card a hinge to disguise what is inside.

✪ Next decorate the front with a red heart from the foil, or whatever else you like.

✪ Cut out a piece of card the same size as the tape box, write your Valentine message on it and slip it in the box facing out.

✪ Stick the tape box inside the card with the pads or tape, slightly nearer the bottom to balance out the weight when it stands up.

It's ready to send — leave it on your Valentine's desk at school. He can slam it in his Walkman!

Quick card number one

Loveheart cards

Just buy some strong card in a bright color (pink would be good!), a box of heart candies, (you may need more), and some clear glue. Make a card shape out of the card and then glue the candy in a pattern on the front. You

could do a heart, your Valentine's initials, or a message. When that has dried, completely cover the front of the card with a layer of clear glue using a paintbrush. This seals the candy in a see-through coating like varnish. Easy or what?

Extremely quick card number two

E-cards

If you have access to the Internet and you know your Valentine's e-mail address, you can call up a search engine and type in "e-card". It will come up with lots of different addresses for sending them. You can also send

virtual flowers from these sites too. Give these a shot:

www.bluemountain.com/eng/valentine/
www.marlo.com/val.htm
www.e-cards.com/occasion/valentines/
www.bemine.com/

What is a friend? A single soul in two bodies. Anon

Groovy gifts

Surprise a friend with a funky present for Valentine's.

Glamorous feather choker

My friend Rachel makes these chokers and they look beautiful.

You will need:

Sequined trim about quarter of an inch (half a centimeter) wide — approximately the length of once around your neck

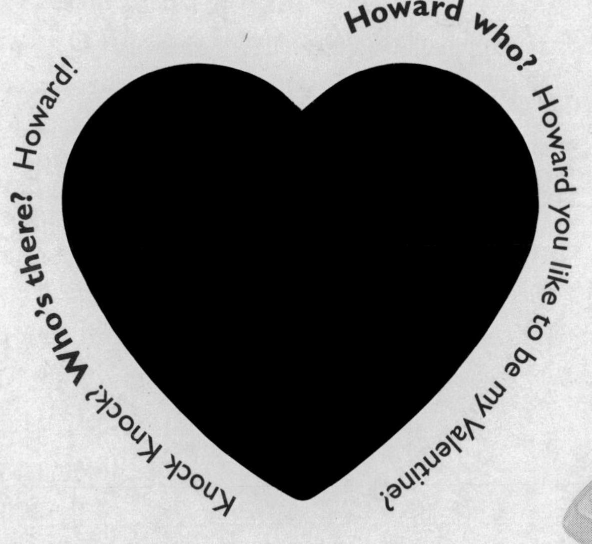

A press stud
Needle and cotton
One or two feathers or a peacock feather for added glamour
Fine fuse wire

❖ Take the sequined trim and measure it around your neck so that it fits quite snug.

Hopefully your friend's neck is the same size. You don't want to strangle her!

❖ Grab the press-stud and sew one half on one end of the trim and the other half on to the other end. This will keep the choker in place on your neck.

❖ Cut two pieces of fuse wire and wind them around the stalk ends of the feathers.

❖ Once the fuse wire has a firm grip on the feathers, you can attach it to the sequined trim. Wind it around a sequin in the center of the trim very carefully. Snip off any extra wire with scissors.

Matching beaded friendship anklet and bracelet

These are so easy to make and are ideal for your Valentine or your friends.

Each one should be different, so to help you make each present individual make them out of the colored beads that best describe your friend or Valentine.

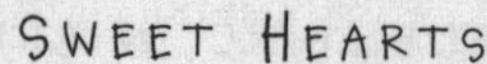

Generous	Orange
Loyal	Blue
Kind	Pink
Responsible	Green
Honest	Red
Cheerful	Yellow

You will need:

Four large colored beads or pony beads (you can choose all different colors or just stick with two and double up)

A length of thin leather string

☆ Cut the leather thread about five inches (twelve centimeters) longer than around your ankle/wrist.

☆ Tie a knot at one end of the string and thread on the four beads.

☆ Thread the other end of the string through the beads from the opposite direction and tie a knot in the end. The size can be adjusted by pulling on the knotted rope ends.

Another idea is to make these as necklaces with names. You can buy beads with letters on them from craft shops and make them for all your friends.

Kool keyrings

You can make all different types of keyrings. Just buy some plain keyrings from a craft store.

Personalized.

You will need:

Four to six inches (Ten to fifteen centimeters) of leather string

Beads with letters on them and other assorted beads

★Tie a knot at one end of the string and thread a bead on to it, right up to the knot. Tie a loop to hook on to the keyring right next to the bead and secure with a double knot.

★ Figure out how much space you have left on the string after you have spelled out the name and make up for it with colored beads.
★Add a few colored beads first and then spell the name and finish with colored beads. Leave enough space to tie a knot at the end.

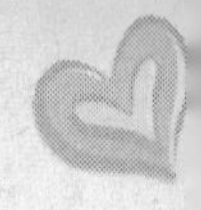

Thread on to the keyring.

Top tip!

For sports fans, spell out the name of their favorite team with the team colors. You will need a longer piece of string and it might be better to do it in two shorter pieces rather than one long one.

To give pleasure to a single heart by a single act is better than a thousand heads bowing in prayer. Ghandi

That quote just about sums up Valentine's day. Giving presents is very rewarding. Now get out there and make, make, make!

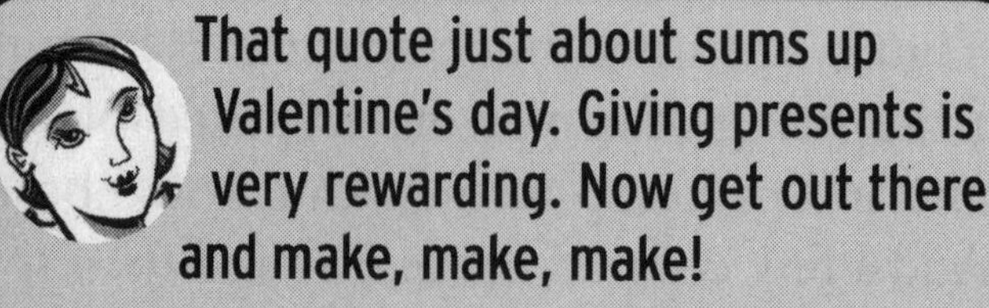

5
All About Me

You know what's more important than being everybody's best friend? You should cuz it's important! You must be happy with yourself, love yourself. I don't mean prancing around

in front of the mirror telling yourself how gorgeous you are, although that's OK sometimes, but having the self-confidence to relax and be completely natural with friends and family. If this is already you, then great! But not everyone can stick their hand up in class and not turn hot pink.

Hey, look at me!

Do this quick confidence quiz and see if you need to read on!

1 You've been invited to a cool party and are getting ready to go. Do you:

(a) Have about five outfit changes cuz you know most of your clothes make you look like a sack of potatoes – honest!?

(b) Decide not to go at the last minute. You are having a bad hair week and want to hide from the world?

(c) Sling on your fave outfit – it always looks great
door excited?

2 When you have to work as a group on a history project, do you:

(a) Think you have some OK ideas and suggest them to the project leader?

(b) Clam up and just listen because you're sure everyone would think your ideas are stupid?

(c) Become project leader right away, because everyone always looks to you for ideas?

3 Whenever you have to speak in front of lots of people, do you:

(a) Feel sick and shaky, but once you've finished you're usually OK?

(b) Curl up and die with all those people looking at you?

(c) Get a real thrill and always volunteer for the school plays?

❹ What do you think is your best feature?

(a) Probably your eyes – everyone is always telling you that!

(b) Possibly your left earlobe, if it's hidden by your hair.

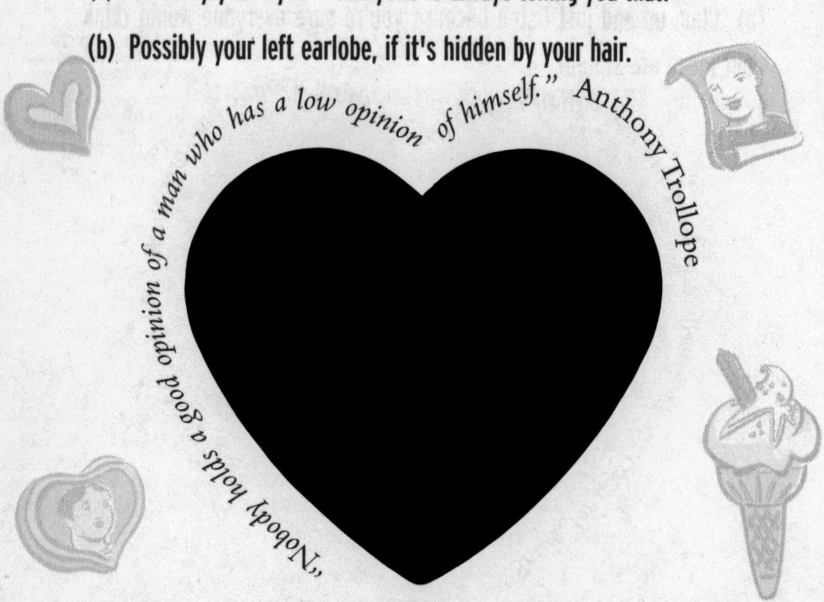

(c) All of you looks fine to you, thanks very much!

❺ Do you worry what people think of you?

(a) Sometimes.

(b) All the time!

(c) Not really, no.

How did you do?

Mostly As

You have self-confidence but can be a tiny bit hard on yourself sometimes. Relax a bit more and remember to enjoy yourself and you will instantly appear more confident. You could do with a few confidence-building tricks, so read on

Mostly Bs

You need to stop worrying about what people think of you all the time.

The world isn't going to end if you speak out once in a while. Read the rest of the chapter and try out some ideas – you never know they might help you see yourself differently.

Mostly Cs

You don't need any help in the confidence department, do you? Good for you, but be careful not to get too bossy – remember, other people aren't as confident as you, so make room for them too.

Confidence tricks

Looking confident makes people think you're confident, so try out a few of these tips . . .

★ When you enter a room where you don't know many people, smile and they will notice you — that way you have no excuse to slide into the background.

★ Next time you have to answer in class and are worried you might have the wrong answer, so what? Is the roof going to cave in? No — I think not!

★ If any boy EVER teases you for being fat (so what if you're not a skinny stick — who is?)

just reply: "At least I can lose weight — what can you do about being ugly?"

★ If you go around thinking you are not as cool/good-looking/trendy/funny/clever as everyone else is, then they will believe you. Pay attention to what you are good at and make that your strong point!

★ Make yourself do one thing a month that really gives you the shakes and clammy hands. Like speaking out, wearing something you'd never normally wear, talking to someone you don't know, going to a party alone, asking people to come to a movie, taking a small part in a school play — anything. And then reward yourself with something you love doing.

You really are GORGEOUS!

Do you think that people who look confident all the time really are? Most models, actresses, and singers have something about themselves that they aren't happy with — no one is perfect.

Everyone has these thoughts, but what people have learned is to make the most of themselves in every way. Take a peek here . . .

If you are worried about:

Skinny legs – you'll look great in flared pants with a low-slung waist.

Stocky legs – wear dark-colored, parallel-legged pants or knee length skirts rather than mini skirts if you are self-conscious about them.

Big hips but small waist – wear fitted A-line skirts or pants that skim your shape. Dark-colored fitted dresses look cool too. Bright-colored tops with detail across your chest or an eye-catching necklace can detract attention from your lower half if you feel self-conscious. Avoid low-waisted pants – they will widen your hips.

Being too short – it is best to wear slip dresses in one color or

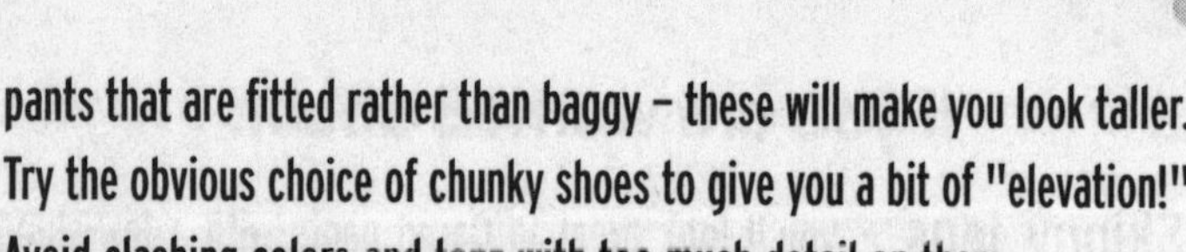

pants that are fitted rather than baggy – these will make you look taller. Try the obvious choice of chunky shoes to give you a bit of "elevation!" Avoid clashing colors and tops with too much detail on them.

Being too tall – wear bright colored tops with detail on the chest, or backless ones with ties at the back to be daring, teamed with straight-legged pants or knee-length skirts. Avoid long outfits in one color – they will make you look even taller!

Having big feet – shoes that aren't too clunky work best with long baggy pants. Avoid platforms with mini skirts!

Dress to really suit you – show off your best features – no more hiding in clothes that do nothing for you or your self confidence.

Other common self-confidence downers you CAN deal with!

My hair is too curly:

Go to a good hairdresser to get it cut and styled, and try hair products to tame those tresses. Ask the hairdresser to show you how

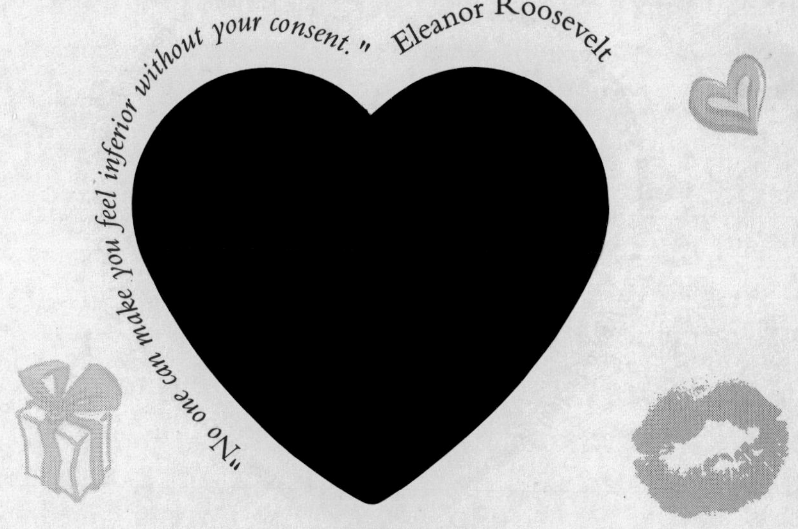

you can recreate the style easily at home without having to stand in front of a mirror for hours each day. Remember — lots of girls would kill for those curls, so make them an asset!

My nose is too big:

Are you sure? It is most likely you who thinks it's too big. Can you hang a coat off it? No? Then it's fine. A good trick is to have your hair cut in a style that makes your face look wider — layered with lots of volume to

help your nose (which isn't too big!) look smaller. Team that with big hoop earrings and blusher on your cheekbones to further widen your face.

My ears stick out:

This is one that everyone has had! Honest!!! You are not alone. BUT, if it really bothers you to the point of distraction, there is only one thing to do — grow your hair over them and avoid ponytails. Soon you will forget they are there!

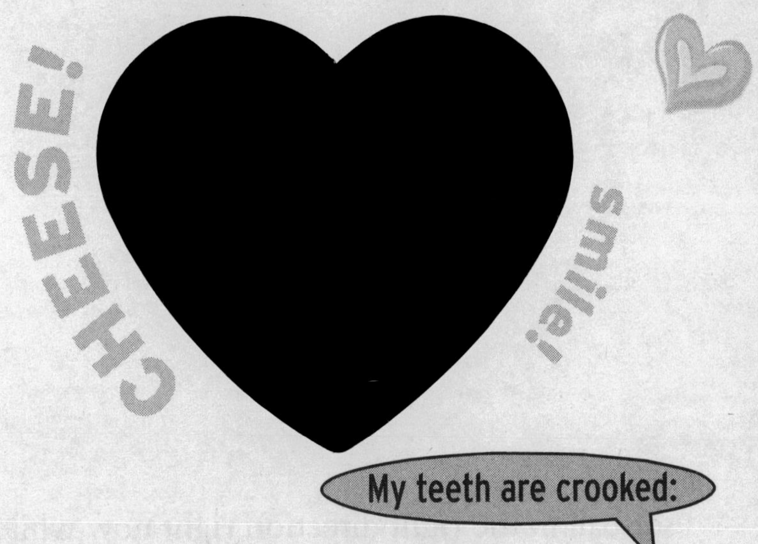

My teeth are crooked:

If they are that bad, your dentist will have given you braces. You can get clear ones now so they don't show. If you really want to draw attention away from your mouth, wear clear or natural lip-gloss. Instead, concentrate your make-up skills on your eyes to make them really stand out.

I'm no good at sports:

Do you think Posh Spice lost sleep about her lack of sporting triumphs at school? No! It may seem important to be able to hit a

softball in the right direction right now while you are at school — but in the real world, no one plays softball unless they really want to. And if you know you'll never want to, then don't let it bother you. Save your energy for stuff you like doing.

I'm the class brain:

Good for you! Keep it up, but remember to have fun occasionally. It can't all be work, work, work. And if people make fun of you, just think forward a few years to when you'll have a highflying job. You have to work hard

to get somewhere in life. Do you think Britney regrets all that time spent working hard to get where she is?

I blush really easily:

This one is a hard thing to combat as it is your body that is making the blood flow to

your skin when you feel awkward or embarrassed. When you know you are going to be in a situation where this might happen — speaking in public, answering a question in class, talking to a boy — pause and take a deep breath. Concentrate on breathing from

the bottom of your tummy while you are talking and the blush should go away as your mind is working on something else. Don't forget to speak though!

Remember that talking about how you feel to a friend, parent, or even the school counsellor can make you feel a lot better. Adults may be a pain sometimes, but they do have some good ideas on how to help you feel better about yourself.

Finally!

Make a list of everything you are good at, and even if you can only think of one thing, make sure you can be the very best you can at it — it may lead to bigger and better things! Trying something new can make you feel like a million bucks. Good luck!

6
Munchie Magic

Food — what a great way to get your friends all in one place at the same time. Frozen meals — take a hike, you want the real thing! Just beg some help from the parents and soon

you could be stuffing food fit for superstars.

But before you even think about food, you have to organize drinks.

Strawberry orange blush

Want to ditch Coke? Try this fruit cocktail.

✤ Wash 8oz (225g) of strawberries then put them in the blender with some ice and the juice of two oranges.

✤ Blend until smooth and serve in tall glasses with orange and strawberry garnishes and little cocktail umbrellas. Oh yes!

Super Shakes

You need to get whizzy with the blender for these.

Chocolate – 10 fl oz (300ml) soft chocolate ice-cream, two tablespoons chocolate-flavored syrup, and 10fl oz (300ml) milk

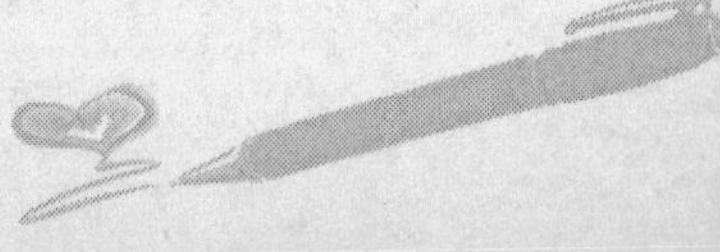

✤ All you need to do is toss it all in the blender and whiz. Serve in tall glasses with chocolate grated on top.

Strawberry – 8oz (225g) washed strawberries, 4fl oz (125ml) vanilla ice-cream or plain/ strawberry yogurt, 10 fl oz (300ml) milk

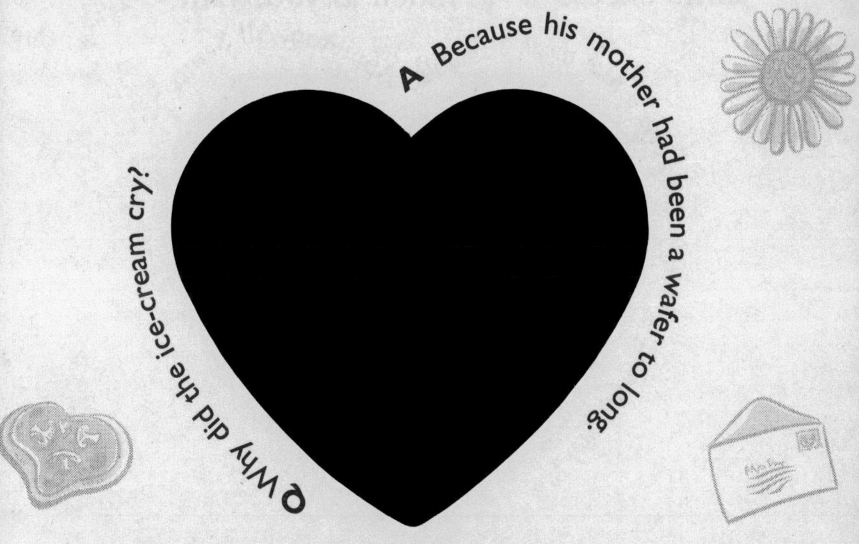

✤ Blend, blend, blend, pour into tall glasses and decorate with slices of strawberries.

Starter

Cheesy Pesto Melts

One French bread loaf

One jar of pesto from the supermarket

Grated mozzarella cheese

❁ Cut the bread into one-inch (three-centimeter) diagonal slices and toast one side under the grill.

❁ Turn over and spread a generous bit of pesto on that side then on top of that put some cheese — as much as you want.

"I love unwinding with friends over a nice meal." Natalie Appleton, All Saints

❁ Put back under the grill and wait until the cheese has started to brown. You will not believe how amazing they taste and they are sooo easy to make.

Main Course

Tomato and red onion tarts

One pack defrosted puff pastry
One tube sundried tomato paste
About fifteen baby tomatoes chopped in half
Two medium red onions cut into rings
Fresh basil to garnish
One egg yolk

❋ Heat the oven to 450°F (230°).

❋ Roll out the pastry into a square until it is about a quarter of an inch (half a centimeter) thick then cut into eight squares and place on a large greased baking sheet. You can eat any leftovers cold.

❋ Score a one-inch (two-centimeter) crust around the edge of each square like a frame and brush it with egg yolk.

❋ Spread an even layer of tomato paste over each of the tart bases keeping within the crust.

Q What is sweet and sour and violent?

A Kung food!

❋ Place the tomatoes with the cut edge facing upward on to the tomato paste. On top of the tomatoes go the onion rings.

❋ Just sprinkle a pinch of salt over them and put them in the oven for about fifteen minutes or until the pastry is golden.

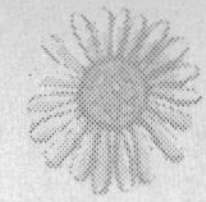

❋ When you take them out the crust will have risen around the tomatoes. Clever — eh? Rip up some basil leaves and sprinkle over each tart.

You might want to serve this with a side order of fries, but not just any old fries. Try these . . .

Spicy fries

You could peel and chop your own fries, but this is easier:

✻ Get a bag of oven fries and tip them into a baking tray. Sprinkle on a teaspoon of cayenne pepper, a teaspoon of paprika, and a teaspoon of garlic powder. Add some

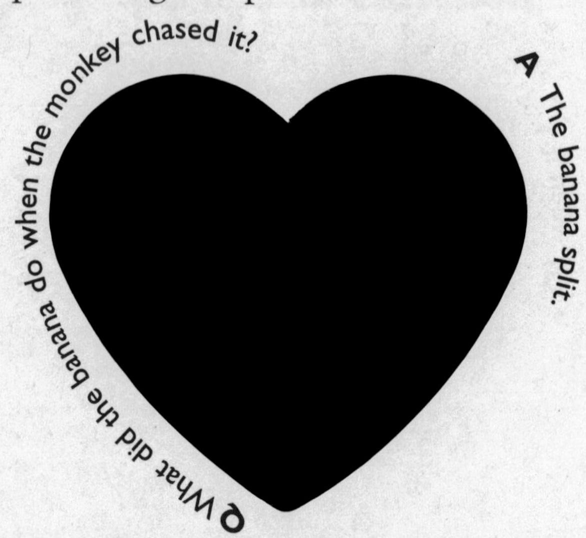

salt and pepper too.

✻ Mix well and make sure all the fries are coated, then put them in the oven and cook as per the oven fries instructions.

Dessert Alert!

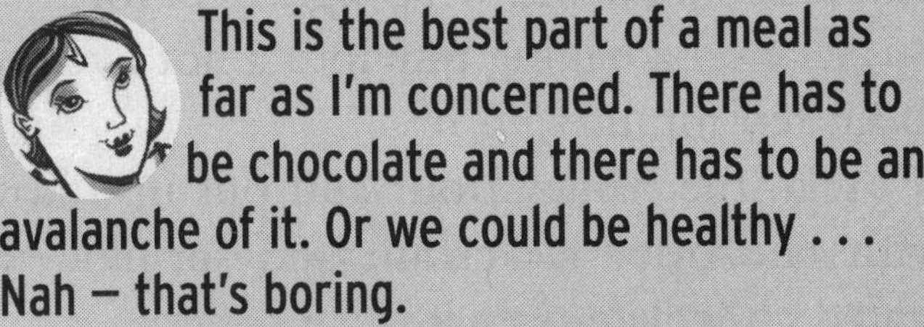

Chocolate banana surprise

Get as many bananas as there are people.
Bags and bags of chocolate chips
Grated chocolate

✲ Slice each banana down the center length-wise then take the chocolate chips and stuff them into the middle. Jam on the other half

of the banana when it looks sufficiently chocolate-filled and wrap tightly in foil.

✲ Place on a baking tray into a hot oven for about ten minutes.

✲ Take the bananas out and put in a bowl with chocolate ice-cream and sprinkle the grated chocolate over it.

Extra quick chocolate goo cake with chocolate sauce

4oz (100g) self-raising flour
4oz (100g) powdered sugar
4oz (100g) softened butter
Two tablespoons of milk
Two eggs

8oz (200g) dark chocolate melted
4oz (100g) milk chocolate melted
5fl oz (150ml) of cream

✲ Preheat the oven to 375°F (170°C). Grease a deep cake pan and line with greaseproof paper.

✲ Grab a grown-up to fix up the food processor and put in the flour, eggs, sugar,

butter, melted chocolate, and milk.

✲ Pour the goo into the cake pan and put it in the oven for about thirty minutes, or until you can pierce it with a skewer and it comes out cleanish — not too dry or it won't be gooey enough.

✻The sauce is easy too. Heat up the cream, but don't let it boil. Add the milk chocolate and stir.

✻ Tip the cake out of the pan and serve in chunks with ice-cream or soft fruit like strawberries or raspberries. Pour sauce over the concoction and dig in.

By now if your friends haven't been sick from all the goo and chocolate, they will be very impressed by your culinary skills. And you should be well on your way to being hostess with the mostess . . .

Mail Mates

What did we do before e-mail? Was there such a time? Oh yeah — snail mail. Well, it still has its uses. You always want to run down stairs on your birthday and wade through a

zillion cards to show how popular you are. BUT, e-mail is the way of the future for keeping in touch with your friends, whether they be on the other side of the planet or around the block. Friendship is like a fish with a bicycle if we can't get in touch — useless. So keep talking . . .

Tips for getting in touch:

★ If you have no e-mail address, but access to the Internet at home or school, get your own free address at **www.hotmail.com** — it's cheaper than calling . . .

★ Send e-cards and virtual presents over the net via e-mail. They are impulsive and you don't have to find a stamp. Some sites have already been covered in the book, but try these for cards and postcards:
www.ecard.corbis.com/
www.americanheart.org/ecard/

www.musicalecards.virtualave.net/
www.cardsAlive.com/
www.arkworld.com/
⋆You can send customized e-notes to e-mail addresses too. It is like a letter, but has music (!) and a layout like cheesy writing paper.

Crack someone up with bunnies and geeky musak — **www.bluemountain.com/**
⋆ Maybe one of your friends or boyfriend would appreciate a supremely sappy personalized poem on e-mail. Is there nothing you can't send? This site **www.netpoets.com** is good for love and friendship poems.

Emoticontastic!

Because it is hard to tell the tone of someone's voice from an e-mail, things can get a bit messy and wires get crossed. So to make what you are saying clearer to your friend, add some emoticons. They can show if you are happy, sad, angry, puzzled, joking,

laughing — the list is endless. Other emoticons can be cartoon characters or describe what you look like. The emoticons are made up of the symbols on your keyboard. The idea is that you look sideways at them to get the meaning.

Take a look at this HUGE collection,

never before seen in one place. Perhaps you can make up your own . . .

:-) I am happy.

:-(I am sad.

;-) I am winking and could be flirting!

:-> I just said something naughty!

>;-> A winking devil – I am evil!

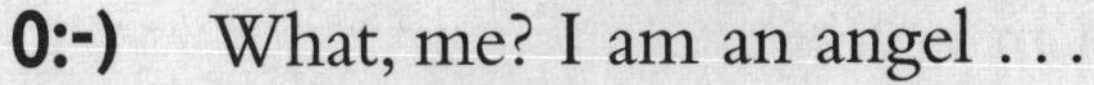

0:-) What, me? I am an angel . . .

:-0 Hoo! I'm shocked.

:^) Profile smiley.

:-P or **:-p** or **:-6** I'm sticking my tongue out.

:-P~~ I'm blowing a raspberry.

:-@ I'm screaming/about to puke.

:-# I wear braces.

8-) or B-) or ::-) I wear glasses.

R-) My glasses are broken.

:-{} I've got lipstick on.

:-* A big smacking kiss.

:-T I'm keeping tight lipped.

:-y I said that with a smile.

:'-(I'm crying.

(:-D Hey – you blabbermouth.

:-& I'm tongue tied.

:-S I just blabbed a lie.

:-/ Yeah – right!

*:o) I'm only joking (clown).

<:-I Sorry, I'm a thicky no brain (dunce).
P-) Hey, I like you, nudge, nudge...
|-) I'm asleep (boredom).
=^.^= a cat
<:3)~~~ a mouse
<+|:) the Pope
[:] Frankenstein

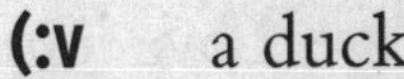

(:v a duck
{(:-) a toupee
7:-) Fred Flintstone
[:-) Walkman

Manic mobiles

If you are lucky enough to have a cell phone, you will know all about the pros and cons of ownership — like the bills, the unproven radiation scares, their stealability. But they make you feel closer to your friends and you can feel safe knowing your old 'rents are only

a phone call away wherever you are. Love 'em or loath 'em, mobile phones are here to stay!

Texting is way cooler than phoning, don't you agree? **See next page . . .**

To text or not to text — the advantages

◆ They are the way to get around the dilemma of making tricky calls to boyfriends in public.

◆ If you are lucky enough to have a cell phone with a vibrating mechanism on it, you can switch it to that and you will feel when you have a message if the phone is near you.

◆ It is cheaper than actually calling your friends.

◆ There are no radiation scares with texting.

◆ You can send romantic messages to your guy, like a card.

◆ You can ask a boy out without the embarrassing call!

Straight to the point!

The only trouble with texting on a mobile is that the keypad is so small, and it can take forever to spell long words. This is where acronyms come in. They have been used on e-mail for years and are made up of the first letter of every word in a well-known phrase.

BBFN	bye bye for now
BFN	bye for now
BTW	by the way
BYKT	but you knew that
CMIIW	correct me if I'm wrong
CUL8R	see you later
EOL	end of lecture

FAQ frequently asked question(s)
FWIW for what it's worth
FYI for your information
IMHO in my humble opinion
IMNSHO in my not so humble opinion

IOW in other words
LOL lots of love/or laughing out loud
MHOTY my hat's off to you
NRN no reply necessary
OTOH on the other hand
ROF rolling on the floor
ROFL rolling on the floor laughing

SITD	still in the dark
TIA	thanks in advance
TIC	tongue in cheek
TTFN	ta ta for now
TTYL	talk to you later
TYVM	thank you very much
WLOL	with lots of love

Now that you have e-mail and texting, there's no need to speak to your friends ever again. As if! Now we have even more ways of talking on Planet Chat for hours on end.

8
Friends Forever?

This is the only true test to see if you are friends who stick together. Unfortunately this isn't a results in five minutes quiz — this is serious stuff. You need to get your closest

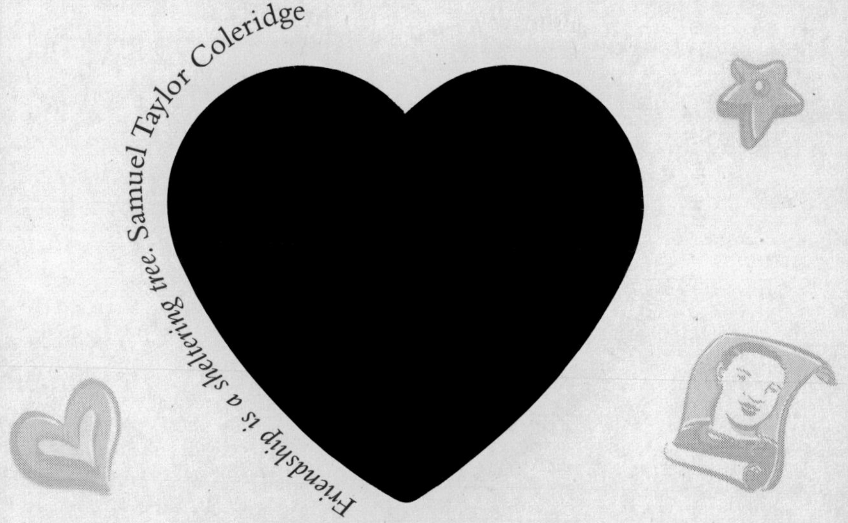

pals all in one place — like a sleepover or something — and make them bring a photo of how they look now. You can photocopy the questionnaire in this book or just use it as an example and make up your own questions. The idea is that one of you pledges to keep all the filled-in questionnaires in a safe place.

How long you keep them is up to you. You might even want to keep them until you are all eighteen as a special coming of age moment. The important thing is that you are all together when you do it. Now it's time to get confessional . . .

My best friend is the man who in wishing me well, wishes it for my sake. Aristotle

About you

Name

____

Age

____

Address

____

This is me

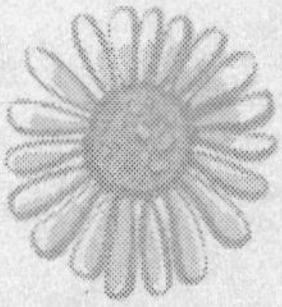

If you won the lottery what would you do with the money?

If you could meet anyone, who would it be and why?

____

____

____

What is the name of your favorite toy?

____

Who is your favorite band or pop star?

____

What is your favorite book?

____

Who are your favorite actor and actress?

____

What about your fave TV program and film?

___

Have you ever been in love?

___

___

Be a friend to yourself, and others will be. Scottish proverb

If you could go anywhere in the whole world, where would that be and why?

___

___

___

___

List your five favorite things

____

____

____

____

____

"The best thing a friend ever did was to save my life." Sophie, 12

Wishes

About your friends

Who is your best friend?

____

What is the best thing they have ever done for you?

____

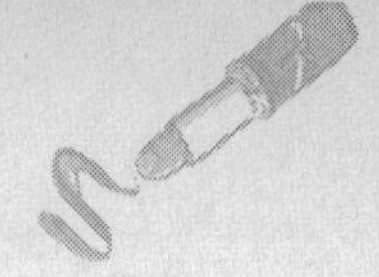

What is the worst thing they have ever done?

"Friends have helped me out with other tricky friendships." Sarah, 11

best friends

Have you ever let a friend down?

Why are friends important?

____

____

____

____

____

"Friends stay forever, boyfriends *come and go.*" Jemima, 14

What is the craziest thing you have ever done with your friends?

____

____

____

____

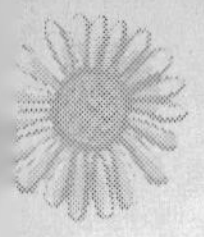

About boys

Boys — cool or a pain? Explain!

"*Friends are people that are like you.*" Jo, 13

FUTURE

Do you have a crush on anyone?

How do you know him?

Are you going out?

____

____

Have you ever kissed a boy?

____

____

____

Who would be your fantasy date and why?

____

____

____

____

____

About the future

How do you think you will have changed from now?

What do you want to be when you get older?

How will you achieve that?

What five things would you like to have done by the time you open this?

____

____

____

____

____

"My mom is my best friend." Simone, 10

FASHION

What makes you think you will still be friends in five year's time?

____

____

____

____

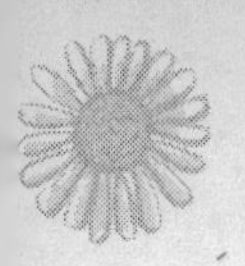

Five things you are most likely to say when you open the box:

1. Ohmigod! Call the fashion police — that shirt is offensive!

2. I can't believe you used to like Matt — he was so gross!

3. Yep — chocolate, still can't live without it.

4. Was that a pattern or had someone puked on your sweater?

5. Boys are still a pain. Will this ever change? (No!)

So that's it. You've filled in your answers and now all you have to do is wait and see if your dreams come true. But in the meantime,

make sure you hold on to your friends because they are an essential ingredient to having fun in the years to come. Without friends there would be no fun, no one to copy homework from or force feed you chocolate when you're so love sick all food sticks in your throat.

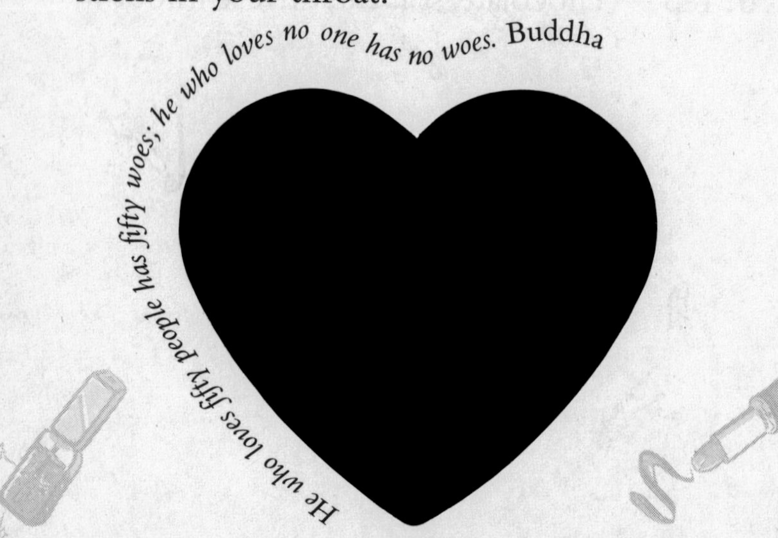

You have been told! You will be surprised how much you will have changed over the years, but one thing will remain the same – the people you call your friends . . .